USGov.Rebuild

FIXES FOR A FAILING GOVERNMENT

Tom Hopper

ACKNOWLEDGEMENTS

To my wife Marilyn, my daughter Karen
and her editor husband Lew Buckley

Foreword

USGOV.REBUILD is the second in the USGOV.FIX series dealing with government. The first was a review of the United States from inception to the present time. That book systematically analyzed the structure and procedures (laws) within which government functions, identified many flaws, and recommended FIXES.

This book addresses two specific issues: institutional leadership and the economy.

TABLE OF CONTENTS
USGOV.REBUILD

CHAPTER 1

The United States in Decline

A woman outside Philadelphia's Independence Hall: Well, Doctor Franklin, what have we got, a Republic or a Monarchy?

Benjamin Franklin: A Republic, if you can keep it.

There are many citizens who believe the United States to be in decline. Nonsense. The Republic is still a developing nation.

The nation is, however, in a period of stagnation brought about by 50 years of inadequate leadership. The increased intransigence in Congress and constant wrangling with the executive branch has caused a consistent erosion in governmental effectiveness, bringing progress almost to a standstill. As an Information Technology pioneer, I worked closely with the Department of Commerce, IBM and AT&T to improve international trade during that period; I experienced the governmental erosion first hand.

After the Iraq fiasco and the 2008 financial meltdown, I determined to find the causes of the erosion. The result was a book called USGOV.FIX, published in 2010 and revised in 2012 to reflect the potential impact of that year's presidential election.

USGOV.FIX reviewed the founders' vision, the institutional government, the growth of the nation and the condition of the country in 2012. The analysis confirmed the obvious economic problems and identified some institutional and economic flaws. The objective of that book was to awaken citizens to the dangers of the present governmental path. My hope was to spur citizens to accept the challenge and take the necessary action steps to FIX the problems identified.

USGOV.REBUILD expands on that effort, concentrating on the institutional government and the economy. For the exercise to be productive, an open citizen mindset is requested. I hope to help people see government as a system. Feeding, sheltering and providing security for three hundred million people is the ultimate systemic challenge. The current stagnation is the result of institutional flaws, exacerbated by inadequate leadership. Corrections will only take place when citizens realize the magnitude of the problem and demand that FIXES be made.

USGOV.REBUILD is the first of the USGOV.FIX supplements dedicated to nation rebuilding. The FIXES recommended in this book are based on my original analysis. If the reader has not read the original USGOV.FIX or wishes for more supporting detail, that book is available on Amazon in both hard copy and Kindle format. Updated information can be found at www.USGovfix.com.

Chapter 2

The Republic

This chapter will encapsulate 225 years of the nation's development, for readers who have not read the 2012 version of USGOV.FIX.

The founders' vision for the new nation was of a representative government of the people. The institutional structure was to be similar to those used in business today. A board of directors would be the policy makers establishing the rules; a chief executive would manage operations; and an audit function would monitor operations and alert the board of directors of deviations so that necessary adjustments could be made.

The result was a Constitution providing an institutional (legal) power base for the new nation. An elected Legislature (Congress) representing the people was assigned primary responsibility for creation of the rules (laws) by which the nation would function. An elected Chief Executive was to manage governmental operations, under the laws created by Congress. The audit function was to be performed by the Supreme Court.

The institutional structure is logically and systemically sound. A major concern of the founders was avoidance of a monarchy, and the separation of powers reflects that intent.

Congress was given primary governmental authority to write its own administrative procedures and to make all laws necessary and proper for carrying into execution the Powers vested by the Constitution. Congress failed in both, resulting in a legal quagmire of laws to manage the nation. This institutional failure created a vacuum allowing the Chief Executive to assume primary governmental control. The nation's development then began to be characterized by a meandering effort based on current political ideology and weakness or strength of the chief executive. Most executives were hostage to a growing political process that gained control of Congress and eventually of government itself.

> *John Adams: "Political parties are to be dreaded as the greatest evil under the Constitution."*

Unfortunately, Adams' concerns were ignored; the result was a nation falling under control of a political process that the quagmire of laws could not contain.

In spite of this anomaly, a great new nation was created. With ingenuity and unlimited natural resources, the U.S.

attained the greatest wealth and power the world has ever known. The country reached its peak in the 1940's, both in the production of armaments and in the military effort necessary to win WWII. On a personal note of pride, the author was a combat soldier in that effort.

After the success of WWII, the nation went into a downward spiral. Congress further exacerbated their primary constitutional failure, thereby increasing the power of the Chief Executive.

The results were catastrophic.

The last fifty years of executive dereliction have included useless and senseless wars, massive debt, flight of industry to other countries, poorly designed and executed social programs, a failing education system and the control of the nation's wealth defaulting to Wall St. The list goes on and on.

Citizens are deeply concerned. They know there is a problem but do not know the solution. The institutional government and the political parties either have no solutions or will not face the issue. The result is a nation in gridlock and stagnation.

Systemically, the way to meet Mr. Franklin's challenge to keep the Republic is to go back to square one and REBUILD the nation according to the founders' vision.

Chapter 3

A Systemic Perspective

Is the prior evaluation overly critical? Let's examine it from a systemic perspective.

The first step in developing any system is establishing its objective(s). The objectives for the new nation were eloquently stated in the Preamble to the Constitution.

We the People of the United States, in Order to form a more perfect Union, establish Justice, insure domestic Tranquility, provide for the common Defence, promote the general Welfare, and secure the Blessings of Liberty to ourselves and our posterity, do ordain and establish this Constitution for the United States of America.

The major step in developing a system is design. Design technology has now become a highly technical profession, creating computer systems, houses, bridges, automobiles and even organizations. Organizational systems are the most complex, and the ultimate challenge is the design of a governmental system. The Constitution represented the founders' systemic design for a Republic. It was a historic first, representing a quantum leap ahead of any governmental concept at that time.

Once system design is complete, the detailed procedures for operations must be written. In Information Technology, these are usually computer programs using logical algorithms supported by procedures for human interaction. For a governmental system, these are legal procedures (laws) that deal with both physical operations and human interaction.

The USGOV.FIX analysis found that the United States governmental system is the best in the world, with one caveat: it operates through an institutional quagmire of procedures (laws) that is inadequate to the needs of the country. Furthermore, these laws have not been updated to keep up with changing requirements.

Failing to develop, enforce and maintain operational procedures will cause any system to erode and eventually fail. By definition, inadequate institutional leadership has allowed this system erosion to happen, if not directly causing it.

CHAPTER 4

The Legal Quagmire

Consider the following judicial paradox: the legal community has dominated our institutional government since its inception, yet our laws are a mess. Currently, sixty percent of the Senate and about forty percent of the House are lawyers, figures that have been relatively constant. One would expect that with so much legal expertise involved in law making, the nation would have an exemplary set of laws to manage the nation. However, nothing could be farther from the truth.

Our legal quagmire is a cloud of legal institutional vapor brought about by incompetent law making. Institutional responsibilities and operational procedures are inadequately defined. The resulting vacuum allows constant wrangling and gridlock within and between governmental branches. This legal mess, whether by design or intent, is what enables the political community to maintain control of government. This state will continue until citizens exercise their constitutional right and demand it be FIXED. Until a firm institutional base is established and definitive responsibilities are enforced, the branches of government will continue to wrangle, stagnation will persist, and the political process will continue to dominate the nation.

Perhaps the greatest danger of our inadequate laws is the pseudo-monarchial control of government it has engendered. Important decisions, like that regarding the Canadian pipeline, are based on political considerations rather than on the good of the nation. Congress has abdicated its institutional role, and the Chief Executive will address only those issues that are politically expedient.

It is unconscionable that the resulting legal quagmire allows political decisions to be made with no regard for the welfare of the nation. Citizens have suffered 50 years of governmental dereliction.

Our institutional government is simply not capable of managing the nation.

CHAPTER 5

Governmental Flaws

The handling of finances is one of the major governmental flaws. The Constitution gave primary fiscal responsibility to Congress. *Congress was to provide the necessary funding, and the Executive branch was to use that funding for day-to-day operations.* Congressional failure and the assumption by the chief executive of the primary role created a schism between the Legislative and Executive branches resulting in persistent intransigence and constrained relations between the two. This flaw has been and remains a major factor leading to our current institutional and economic stagnation.

Is the constant tension between the Legislative and Executive branches a Constitutional flaw? Was the assumption of primary governmental power by the chief executive necessary and beneficial? In the last fifty years, few chief executives have crossed the aisle and worked with Congress.

Does this represent a condemnation of Congress, the Chief Executive or both? The reader/citizen must decide.

This financial schism is not just an example of failure but of a specific institutional flaw that must be corrected. It will *not* be fixed by an ingrained government; it will only be FIXED by a concerned citizenry.

CHAPTER 6

The Constitution

Is the Constitution adequate for the 21st century? This is a valid question.

The Constitution was written in 1776 for a new nation of a few million people. The founders were citizens whose legal backgrounds were based mostly on English law. The structure of the new Constitution was highly influenced by the French revolution and governmental visionaries of that time. Heavily based on Christian principles, it represented a significant breakthrough in political systems.

The institutional base, consisting of the Legislative, Executive and Judiciary branches, is as solid for 2013 as it was for 1776. The supporting procedural base (laws) developed by an incompetent Congress is not.

The Republic as a governmental system is the best in the world; building on that base should be continued. There are some necessary FIXES that can be accomplished through constitutional amendments.

In addition to institutional need, the challenge for the new nation was and is to develop a stable economic base. The institutional branches have not been capable of coordinating their actions to meet the economic needs of the nation, as the 2008 financial meltdown and the huge national debt make clear.

The United States is the greatest nation in the world, but it has both institutional and economic flaws which require FIXES if the Republic is to reach its full potential.

CHAPTER 7

Nation Rebuilding

To begin rebuilding, it is essential to reconfirm the founders' vision of a Republic. The institutional structure of the Republic is the best in the world and must be maintained.

The founders' vision was based on a primarily agricultural nation. The industrial revolution was an unexpected phenomenon and a major factor in the nation's empirical growth. In spite of this radical change, the nation our forefathers created became the greatest nation in the history of the world. It was an effective validation of the founders' vision for a Republic. That vision is as valid today as it was in 1776.

To confirm the validity of that observation, we will reflect briefly on government forms and their socio/economic perspectives. An analysis of our representative government and others confirms that any type of government can function. It also confirms that the quality of performance and the ultimate survival of any nation are dependent on its systemic base.

There are many types and forms of government that offer various degrees of social support. The most significant is Communism, which is theoretically the ultimate form of socialism. It is also a systemic failure, as was proven in Russia and China. China has since converted to a free enterprise oligarchy, while maintaining an ostensibly Communist façade.

Civilization has seen every form of government and social philosophy. Some governments offering strong social support have succeeded, while other similar governments face bankruptcy. Norway and Greece are examples at both ends of the spectrum.

Volumes have been written on government types and forms. The USGOV.FIX evaluation confirmed that the Republic envisioned by our founders is the most effective form of government in the world. The new nation created a homogenous citizenry never before achieved and the greatest wealth and power the world has ever known.

However, this is a critical time for the nation. FIXES must be made to return the nation to its former progressive role. Continuation on the present path will bring bankruptcy and/or the threat of an ideological takeover. There are radical elements that would change our system of government. For most citizens, considering their grandchildren living in any governmental system other than the Republic is unthinkable.

So what is the strategy to rebuild the nation and insure that the Republic remains strong?

The initial phase should be stabilization. We should rebuild on the present base. The government is too fragile and the risk too great for extreme changes.

Stabilization Objectives:

The first objective should be stabilizing the institutional base with necessary amendments to the original Constitution.

Second should be developing a new and stable economy.

The third should be restraint of the political process. The objective of the process is to provide adequate leadership candidates for representation, not to assume overall control of government. The political process is the method by which citizens organize to choose their leaders, *not* the basis by which government functions.

A potential fourth objective could be, to the degree possible, anticipating future requirements and integrating those with the stabilization project for smooth incorporation over time.

My single input for a future objective: government should be *de*centralized under citizen control to the lowest possible functional level. The centralized government has been an abysmal failure.

Note: Constructive rebuilding of the nation can only be done with realistic FIXES. Patchwork expediencies by the political establishment currently in control of government will cause further erosion and almost certain chaos. There is no individual or group in the institutional government capable of rebuilding the nation; this rebuilding must be accomplished by concerned citizens.

Let us now review the institutional branches and their performance.

Chapter 8

The Executive Branch

The increased power of the chief executive was the primary concern identified in USGOV.FIX. The founders' fear of creating a monarchy is being validated.

The chief executive has become a titular world leader with more power than any monarch who ever lived. The major symptoms of this have been senseless wars costing trillions of dollars and thousands of lives. The fact that a vapid Congress approved these disastrous decisions in no way mitigates executive actions.

The executive role as discussed in Chapter 2 has been the key factor in the development of the new nation. After Congress's initial failure to carry out their primary responsibility, the nation developed around the ideology and weakness or strength of the chief executive. My observation is that there have been a few good executives; most were muddlers, and some were abject failures.

The last fifty years seems to have created candidates at the lower end of the spectrum, a trend that has accelerated in the new century. One might expect that within the political process, selection of candidates might show a normal distribution of quality. However, the undeniable fact is that the current stagnation is the result of inadequate executive leadership at both ends of the political spectrum.

A decisive leader is necessary to manage the most powerful and wealthy nation in the world; but if political motivation and global recognition are the primary objectives of the chief executive, the nation is in jeopardy.

The increased power of the chief executive is following a dangerous trend towards monarchy. If institutional responsibilities are not clarified, that trend will continue.

CHAPTER 9

Congress

Congress is unquestionably the weakest member of institutional government. Constitutionally assigned as the nation's lawmakers, Congress has created a legal quagmire to manage the nation. This has allowed the erosion of purpose that has led to the current stagnation. Congress is an ingrained clique whose seniority system provides the base for dynasties. They maintain political life-and-death control over their members, and their loyalties to their ideologies far outweigh those to the nation. Law making is totally political and self-aggrandizing. From their assigned primary Constitutional role, they have denigrated to an actual impediment to reaching the ultimate potential of the Republic.

Readers who think this is a scathing indictment should read or reread the original USGOV.FIX analysis.

A major concern is the internal politicking brought about by the concentrated power base. The Washington establishment mirrors the corrupt courts of historical monarchs, the primary difference being that the monarch could chop off a few heads when necessary to maintain balance and control.

Another pathetic failure is domination by a lobbyist community that has taken over Congress and spends 3 billion dollars a year on influence peddling. They are even allowed to write or modify laws for the benefit of their clients. It's a question of whether earmarks or lobbyist activities are the more corrupting factors. All of this is made worse by the "revolving door" syndrome; many members of Congress become lobbyists upon leaving Congress.

The major systemic question for Congress is the logic of a representative body of citizens being organized by political ideology. The original rationale for the split organization was to coordinate the diverse requirements of individual members, each of whom had their own agenda. This did not resolve the issue; decision-making still had to be further relegated to committees. Systemically, I would question why organization by states would not provide better representation? It would open the door for improved voting options that have always been a bone of contention between large and small states. Shared Committee assignments could provide an adequate level of shared ideological influence.

The undeniable fact is that the decision to create a politically organized body created an atmosphere that encouraged the intransigence between parties that has resulted in institutional gridlock and governmental stagnation.

Finally and most important, the ideological split is a dominant factor in political control of government. The Republic will never realize it's full potential with the institutional government under political control. Congress is the major culprit in this malfunction.

I recommend going back to the drawing board regarding the Congress; every aspect of its institutional responsibility needs to be reviewed.

CHAPTER 10

The Judiciary and the Legal Community

The Judiciary, though marginally more competent than the Congress, has still failed to fulfill its vested responsibilities. Systemically, it is difficult to define their scope and limits. Since all judgments reach across the spectrum from the lowest to the highest level of human behavior, they set the standards for citizen interaction. As such, the Judiciary should reflect the moral fiber of the nation. As the highest level of legal authority they should set the standards for the legal community and law making.

The legal community has dominated government since inception, but they have never reached the professional level required to allow the Republic to attain its full potential. The quagmire of laws the nation lives under is the result of not only incompetence, but also of apathy. Members of the legal community live in a separate world, speak their own language, and surround themselves with massive, heavily laden bookshelves to perpetuate an aura of omnipotence.

Their omnipotence does not, however, keep them from using yellow pages and TV ads to line their pockets or using the court system for processing claims that add to the costs of social services. Medical and other costs are inflated by the necessary insurance for social workers against ridiculous legal claims. The cost of their "omnipotence" is about $5000 a year for the average American family.

The legal community has made no attempts to improve the quality of their profession, and the judiciary has not lived up to the honorable status it was vested in by the Constitution.

CHAPTER 11

Institutional Fixes

The first FIX will begin with the institutional government.

The recommended institutional FIX is an in-depth analysis and role definition of the three branches of government.

From this analysis, precise rules of the institutional branches' duties and limits thereto can be established. Constitutional amendments with explicit definition of each branch's responsibility can be adopted. Detailed operational procedures (laws) can then be provided for ongoing operations. The legal quagmire can be cleaned up, the constant bickering as to responsibility can end, and gridlock can be eliminated.

The major emphasis in the executive review would be to address the issue of governmental authority and limits thereto.

Does the Legislative or the Executive branch have
primary governmental authority?

Gridlock is destroying the nation. If the primary governmental power is in the Legislature, we have a Republic. If it is in the Chief Executive, we have a pseudo-monarchy. This institutional vacuum has allowed the continued erosion of governmental effectiveness, leading to the current stagnation.

The Congressional branch review should address the legal quagmire and governmental lawmaking procedures.

The analysis should also include the possible reorganization of Congress to a state base rather than the current political base. Given the huge differentials in population, state representation has always been questionable; improved methodology for representation would be possible.

The study should also address the bicameral structure. Does the nation need two separate law making bodies? Was the founders' decision for two bodies to further enforce a balance of power? If so, it failed. Would a smaller legislative body be more effective? The rules defined in 1776 were shaped on the logistical and administrative limits of that time. With Information Technology and the new media, there are no limits; all options should be on the table.

The congressional review should include moving the legislative function back to the states. With today's media technology, the function could be performed remotely and almost certainly more effectively. Getting the legislative function away from the Washington establishment and the lobbyists would have tremendous benefits. In any event, the entire lawmaking process must be completely transparent and designed so that it could be decentralized quickly with limited disruption. Given our current state of worldwide terrorism, a distributed government may be required for security reasons.

The judicial branch review should confirm that the mechanics of government do not supersede the objectives of the Republic as stated in the Preamble to the Constitution. The moral fiber of the nation requires that laws should be adopted to confirm citizens' inalienable rights. Perhaps as importantly, laws should also define citizens' responsibility.

Citizens' responsibility to the nation has never been defined. The nation has endured every possible form of exploitation, but strong ethical principles have allowed it to survive. That national ethic was nurtured in the home and in the community. Citizens' responsibilities were never formalized in the legal quagmire, and rogue citizens have taken advantage of that vacuum with terrible consequences.

The legal quagmire must be cleaned up, incorporating pro-cedures (laws) with precise definition of citizen responsibil-ity to the nation and penalties for dereliction. This should apply to every citizen, whether acting individually or as part of a larger organization.

In support of this position, suffice it to say there must nev-er be another national exploitation like the 2008 financial meltdown, which virtually destroyed the middle class and nearly bankrupted the nation.

The magnitude and scope of the recommended institution-al analysis is beyond the capability of existing members. It cannot be done on an ad hoc basis. A professional task force incorporating the nation's most qualified Information Technology, organizational, and legal expertise will be required.

The project should have Congressional sponsorship. Retired bipartisan government leaders would be an ex-cellent sounding board. Select members of the academic community might be persuaded to leave their ivy cloisters and pitch in.

Finally, a major objective should be wresting political con-trol from the current government and returning it to the people. Political payback must be eliminated. The purpose of political parties is to provide candidates for Legislative and Executive leadership, not to use politics as a means to dominate the nation. The Republic cannot survive if governmental function, rather than merely the process of choosing candidates, is controlled by the political process.

Great caution is required. The project deliverable from the institutional analysis must include a detailed plan to handle any recommended governmental restructuring. The current government is too fragile for extreme changes.

We will now move on to review short-term flaws that have led to the current institutional stagnation.

Chapter 12

Institutional Stagnation

While the institutional analysis is being carried out, we should begin governmental stabilization by addressing three major flaws identified in the USGOV.FIX analysis.

The first flaw we should address is in the electoral process.

> *This egregious process regularly disenfranchises 80% of the population and is a major factor in political control of government. It also opens the door for fiascos such as the 2000 Florida chad debacle allowing an executive to win by a few hundred votes.*

The next flaw to be addressed is in the destabilizing effect of national elections.

> *Elections create massive disturbances in both the economy and the social community. The elector community and campaign contributions must be re-evaluated.*

The final flaw is in the political process.

> *Through the use of payback, the political pro-*
> *cess has effectively taken over the institutional*
> *government.*

These very obvious flaws are identified in the original USGOV. FIX analysis. Let us discuss them in more detail.

CHAPTER 13

The Electoral Process

The pros and cons of using a state-based electoral process for selection of the chief executive represent a long-standing controversy. This topic has been treated mostly with lip service, never achieving the significant treatment it deserves. Critical mass has now been reached with the Supreme Court's removal of contribution restrictions to Super PACs. Citizen representation has been eroded if not altogether lost. Settling this controversy and developing an improved electoral process are top priorities that can no longer be ignored.

Past opponents of electoral change have dismissed it as a placebo that would probably not impact the election results.

> *The purveyors of this objection, either by intent or ignorance, completely miss the point. The state-based electoral process has virtually destroyed citizen selection of the chief executive.*

If the process is allowed to continue, an elite community with Super PAC funding may well rule the nation. The Chief Executive would become a titular monarch under a façade of democracy. Citizens would lose their voice, and the Republic would degrade or disappear entirely.

Electing the Chief Executive through a majority citizen vote is often promoted for change, but this would be a poor option. A majority citizen vote would in fact allow more political chicanery than the current state-based process. It would also cause all sorts of citizen strife, as political hacks play ethnic, race, religious and other factions against each other. A majority citizen vote for President would fracture the homogenous community built through centuries of commitment and sharing.

The electoral process is a critical issue, and it must be changed. It is a major power source of the political community. It was a reasonable solution when conceived, but it has long since outgrown its relevance.

CHAPTER 14

The Election Trauma

What is the electorate, and how are elections funded?

The electorate is made up of qualified citizens who use their votes to choose governmental leadership. Campaign funding is the methodology used to pay the costs of candidates' campaigns for office.

The election trauma is another of the institutional flaws identified in the original analysis. The flaw is the disruptive impact of national elections. National elections have become a major disturbance to the nation. The political hype blurs all reason, and the media blitz outweighs all other news.

The carnival tactics and the associated media hype that have become part and parcel of the political process create economic and social chaos. These disturbances exacerbate the inherent economic swings of a dynamic industrial nation. Political maneuvering results in delays of critical national decisions. Maintaining economic and social stability is virtually impossible, and citizens live in a constant state of anxiety.

The most impactful flaw is the four-year presidential election. Choosing a new Chief Executive, the entire House of Representatives and a third of the Senate all at the same time is hugely disruptive. A change of this magnitude in political control throws the institutional government and the nation into chaos.

The Supreme Court decision to allow unlimited campaign contributions from the commercial community exacerbates the problem, virtually destroying citizen representation. The entire process is an affront to dedicated citizens.

No system can achieve any level of stability when the base is subjected to such extreme disturbances. The constitutional decisions made in 1776 regarding elections were valid at that time. However, this is no longer 1776; our elections, based on those decisions, now result in disturbances that are counterproductive to the growth of the nation and the requirements of our massive socio-economic system.

These disturbances can no longer be tolerated.

CHAPTER 15

The Political Process

The political process, supposedly merely a tool for choosing our representative leaders, has now taken over the institutional government. Through the use of political payback, this process has taken over the reins of government.

Sharply divided political ideologies have created intransigent malevolent forces, threatening the Republic. Governmental decisions are based on the impact to the political party in power; the welfare of the nation becomes secondary.

The focus of both parties is to win elections by whatever means necessary. The qualifications of the candidates are incidental to their chances of winning. The resulting carnival scenario is an affront to every dedicated citizen and is a demeaning exhibition before the rest of the world.

Leadership selection through the political process has been an abject failure. Its only redeeming feature is that the two parties (ostensibly conservatives and liberals) provide a balance, offsetting each other. This alone has kept the nation from debilitating to a pure monarchy or a socialist state. Alternative options for leadership selection should be explored, but until a better solution is found we will have to live with it. In the meantime, the recommended FIXES will hopefully mitigate the political process' destructive tendencies.

CHAPTER 16

The Electoral Process FIX

This FIX addresses the egregious state-based electoral process that regularly disenfranchises 80% of citizens in presidential elections.

> *The recommended FIX for presidential selection is to make the winning candidate the one who wins a majority of the Congressional Districts.*

This change would resolve the illogical anomaly that Congressional Districts are the basis for choosing legislators but are ignored in the selection of the Chief Executive. With Congressional Districts as the electoral base, House members would move into the main stream. They would become more effective in their districts and increase their clout in Washington. They would become dynamic fighters for selection of the most capable candidates for the Presidency. An incumbent or potential future Chief Executive could no longer ignore this powerful representative base.

With this change, the political process would no longer depend on the swing state aberration for victory. There is little probability that political chicanery could manipulate 435 Districts as it now can manipulate 10 or 11 swing states.

The need for the best possible system for selection of executive leadership is critical. The Congressional District recommendation is a logical step that would be easy to implement. It should strengthen the current fragile government.

The electoral process is *the* major power source of the political community; it must be changed.

The following FIXES are directed at the election process.

The electoral process has major representative flaws that must be corrected.

> *The FIX: Modify the electoral process so that the Presidential election would be determined by the most Congressional Districts won.*

The Republic is a representative government of the people. Citizen representation is destroyed by non-elector campaign contributions to official candidates.

> *The FIX: Limit campaign contributions to electors only, with set maximum contributions.*

The two- and four-year election cycles create massive disturbances to the nation and its citizens. This FIX is to modify the term of the Chief Executive.

The FIX: Establish a single seven-year term for the Chief Executive.

The current two-year term for House Members is a critical flaw. The next two FIXES would build a stronger and more cohesive law making base.

The FIXES: (1) Extend the term of House Members to six years, as in the Senate; and
(2) Limit all Members of Congress to two terms.

Lobbyists spend about 3 billion dollars a year peddling influence with the Washington establishment.

The FIX: Prohibit retired Members of Congress from becoming lobbyists.

The final election FIX is to smooth out the disturbances from the two- and four-year election cycles.

The FIX: Elect one-third of the House and the Senate every two years.

These FIXES sound rather massive, but all are very logical and necessary. Their implementation would go a long way toward stabilizing government and defanging the political monster that now dominates our government and all major policy decisions.

Chapter 18

The Political FIX

Much of the FIX for the political process has been encompassed in the two prior chapters.

FIXING the electoral process will reduce much of the political power. The state-based process allows the focusing of a huge concentration of effort on a relatively small target. Having to address 435 districts would completely change the dynamic.

The changes to election scheduling would also have significant impact. The change to a single seven-year presidential term would result in a near hiatus for the political process. The cycle for Congress, particularly with the six-year term for House members, would stabilize and minimize the disruptive impact of elections.

If it can be accomplished, the elimination of non-citizen campaign contributions would have a major positive impact. The billion dollar campaigns that now cause such a disturbance would be downsized, and a reasonable level of intelligence would be restored to the process.

The two-term limit for Members of Congress would also change the dynamic, taking away the political clout inherent in long-term Congressional dynasties.

If the proposed institutional analysis supports the change to Congressional District based presidential elections, the elimination of political control of government would be largely accomplished.

The ideological perspective should be a positive force for the Nation; opposing ideological forces provide a balance that is critical to stability. The political process has much to offer, but the idiotic tactics currently employed and the resultant gridlock have denigrated this process beyond all reason.

CHAPTER 19

Institutional Critique

The background presented so far has, I think, been accurate. The flaws, both basic and immediate, have been identified. The overall institutional review that is recommended will confirm or reject the perceptions of basic governmental flaws. If the flaws are confirmed and FIXED, there will be a profound impact on the governmental structure, requiring very sensitive reconstruction efforts. Even if the review does not confirm the presence of such flaws, I'm sure the results still would be positive, as the very act of reviewing the process would force government to "clean up its act."

The more immediate flaws leading to the current stagnation can be assessed, and if confirmed, viable action steps can be taken while the overall analysis is continuing. Constitutional amendments will be required for the election FIXES, but I think those will be closely follow any future recommendations from the overall study.

I think the important thing is that citizens adopt a realistic mindset. We should go back to basics and recognize the historical significance of the original Constitution. At the time of its writing, most of the world was still ruled by monarchs. Louis XVI was still on the throne in France; Peter III of Russia had just been deposed in 1762; and George III, from whom we wrested our nation, was on the throne in Britain.

There is no way that a group of citizens in 1776 could write a Constitution that could specifically manage every aspect of a developing nation for 250 years. We must all realize that the laws we live under were not specifically defined in the Constitution; they are based on Congress' interpretation of the Constitution. Those who thump the Constitution for their "inalienable rights" should re-examine that remarkable document to see what it actually says.

Another factor regarding citizen mindset is the moral fiber of the nation. The FIXES identified in prior chapters deal primarily with the mechanics of government. It is critical that mechanics do not supersede the objectives of the Republic as outlined in the Preamble to the Constitution.

Perhaps more importantly, laws should also define citizens responsibility and disciplinary steps to be taken for violators, as stated earlier.

As has often been said, the Republic is the best government in the world. However, as with all things, time takes its toll; the Constitution needs to be re-examined and changed as necessary to remain a growing document.

CHAPTER 20

The Economy

Providing a stable and effective economy has been one of the nation's greatest failures and must be a major thrust in rebuilding.

So why has the United States not been able to establish a viable economy? The answer is a corollary to institutional failure. The politically controlled government has never shown any effort to stabilize the financial universe or even the nation for that matter. The free enterprise economy has been a boom and bust phenomenon from its inception.

The Great Depression finally created such turmoil that government had to take action. Guaranteeing bank deposits was a positive move. The Social Security system was established, which was the beginning of substantial social reforms. These were expanded in the 1960's and have been drastically expanded again in the current administration.

The nation and the economy peaked in the 1940's. Following WWII, the nation lost its way. The wealth creating industrial dynamo was shattered, industry fled overseas, the impending oil crisis was ignored, and social needs exploded. Short-term financial gains became the objective, and the constitutional vision was ignored. An inadequate Government could not or would not face the issues and stood pitifully by as fifty years of erosion wasted much of the nation's wealth.

The seeds for a financial meltdown and the current stagnation were being planted.

Chapter 21

The Financial Meltdown

We've clearly defined our country's failed institutional and economic leadership. Out of this we can define the current crisis. The quagmire of laws written during the empirical, haphazard growth of the nation provided the opportunity for all sorts of financial chicanery. Early schemes involved watering stocks to defraud innocent citizens. In the past fifty years, financial chicanery has been escalated to a new level, as government printing presses have diluted the value of the nation's money.

Money was developed as a medium of exchange and a mechanism for bartering. It was intended to be representative of value, as in a bushel of wheat or a barrel of oil. With fiscal failure, the government has turned money into a commodity. This completely changes the dynamics in the use of money. Banks, as the warehouses of money, profit from financial manipulation rather than investing in wealth-creating ventures. The result is continued dilution of monetary value and tremendous overhead in banking costs. Banking, which should be a primary service function, has become a dominant and counterproductive force in the nation's economy.

> *Thomas Jefferson: I believe that banking institutions are more dangerous to our liberties than standing armies.*

Despite Jefferson's warning, government has never been able to control the nation's finances. As a matter of fact, there are no indications that they ever tried. The nation's wealth was and still is dominated by the banking community. The 1990 decision to let banks operate across state lines opened the floodgates, allowing banks to gain complete control of the economy. The nation's wealth was consolidated under the control of a few banks that were "too big to fail".

The resultant 2008 meltdown came about through a combination of governmental dereliction, deregulation, shadow banking and every imaginable misuse of money. Systemically, the nation's financial structure was shattered.

The meltdown allowed an elite few to accumulate (not create) wealth by skimming the watered money and turning the vapor to wealth by buying real, valued assets. In 2008 the watered money became so much froth that the bubble burst and the nation was thrown to near insolvency. Citizens had to bail out the economy. The wealthy survived while average citizens lost their homes, their pensions and their jobs.

It was the most savage citizen exploitation in the nation's history, and government stood helplessly by.

The frightening part is that no disciplinary or corrective actions have been taken. The perpetrators of the meltdown are still in power, and the risk is still there.

The ultimate citizen humiliation? A large portion of citizens' bailout money was handed over to the meltdown perpetrators as a bonus. It was a national stigma that defies all efforts to describe.

The result has completely disrupted the economy. In the past, middle class citizens purchased homes to raise their families and to build equity that could be used later to assist with retirement. This option has been essentially lost through financial exploitation. The middle class was virtually destroyed.

I am reminded of a business trip to Venezuela in the 1970's. Similar to our country today, 2% of their citizens owned 98 per cent of the wealth. Caracas itself is a beautiful city; but in the surrounding hills, one could see tin shanties that housed three to four million people. It was typical fourth or fifth world conditions, open sewers, etc. I can't help thinking about the trend in civilization. Wealth originally belonged to a few, but over time, social changes caused a distribution of wealth to the population. Is that role reversing again?

Wealth is a necessary ingredient to a growing and vigorous economy. The wealth created by our forefathers through ingenuity and hard work was the substance of the great country we live in. That substance has been turned into froth by inadequate leadership. The money that should be the base on which to maintain the nation's infrastructure has vaporized. The results are a failing educational system, roads and bridges falling apart, and government on the verge of bankruptcy. Our once invincible dollar is eroding in the world marketplace.

Then there is the backlash. The meltdown caused the recession, but the stagnation was exacerbated as the result of government's printing money in an effort to reactivate the economy. Was the recovery effort more destructive than the failure?

I am sorry to put readers through this pathetic review, but citizens must understand the abject failure of the institutional government in managing the nation's finances. The nation cannot survive with that poor quality of leadership. Another meltdown could well destroy the Republic.

CHAPTER 22

Financial Rebuilding Strategy

The Republic was originally built by a globally independent and dedicated community. Iron ore was converted to steel for building and tools; the land provided both food and cotton for clothing; oil became the lubricant for a growing mobile economy. An eager work force rolled up its sleeves and labored long and hard, creating the greatest nation in the world. America became the leader in world commerce, with the greatest wealth the world has ever known.

Commercial dominance and wealth is eroding, and the nation is facing and will continue to face strong competition in the global market place. The wealth-creating engine will be challenged, but it can rise to meet the need if a stable economic base can be re-established.

The resources for global independence are still there. New sources of energy are being found that should handle our needs for decades. With an adequate economic base, there is every chance for a complete national recovery.

As a matter of fact, there are great opportunities ahead. Within this century, world growth will change the global picture completely. Emerging nations will require a high level of industrial and technological support, and our know-how is the best in the world. Increasing populations means an ever-increasing need for food, which will ultimately re-place oil as the predominant factor in global commerce.

Food is important, but it is only one part of the future equa-tion. To prepare for the future, the nation must develop the most efficient and effective uses of all its resources. In a world being torn apart by ethnic and racial violence, any nation must be able to survive on its own resources. Our nation barely survived the oil crisis of the 1970's, and the drastic impact on our economy was and is an alert to the gravity of dependency.

If we are to rebuild our global market, we must consider a major strategic factor called "state capitalism. The term was initiated primarily for the industrial communities creating goods for export. Governments like North Korea have an integral relationship with industry. To what degree should our government intervene with industry or other wealth-creating enterprises?

We will be reviewing this later in discussions on a new econ-omy. For now, suffice it to say that government and wealth-creating enterprises must work together. Government's role should be to provide the necessary ingredients, such as raw materials and energy. The wealth-creating dynamo that has proven itself as the best in world must be supported in every way.

I bring this up at this time to emphasize the advantage the United States has in the global market place. Emerging nations have significant problems with poverty and corruption. They face decades of change before reaching social equality. The United States is a quantum leap ahead of any other nation in social harmony. Other than Congressional earmarks and lobbyists' shameful tactics, we have little corruption. While our labor costs are higher than developing nations, they will eventually reach some degree of parity. Labor costs in China are already escalating. In the long term, US commerce has the greatest potential in the world.

WWII involved a herculean intervention effort that involved creating the tools necessary to win a war in a way that should be a model for the future. National synergy created the most effective and efficient supply system in the history of mankind. That same synergy is needed to again make full use of the nation's resources. The United States did it then and can do it again.

There will be one significant and necessary change, and that is in national planning. The planning strategy should be for government to guarantee that enterprise needs are adequately met and easily accessible. This will allow the commercial community to move full speed ahead. The productivity and resiliency of the past must not be impeded in any way.

National planning will provide a new economic base. A realistic economic model can be developed to optimize all of the nation's resources. This will include energy requirements, obtaining and storage of raw materials (including strategic imports), distribution of goods and services and any other commercial needs. Citizens should be aware that China is well ahead of the United States in this area. National planning, particularly for the long term, is a critical component.

There is another perspective on national planning which must be evaluated. In the 1960's, the Japanese adapted a method called JIT (just in time) manufacturing. This technique was studied in the US but was rejected by industry in that period of stagnation. JIT was very effective in streamlining the movement of materials to the production line. But we saw in the recent Japanese tsunami the negative side of the equation. Production of goods was substantially impaired while supply lines were being restored.

I have long been concerned about a recovery in the US from any major disaster. The trauma brought about by the Hurricane Katrina in New Orleans showed all too well our weakness in this area. A strategic governmental decision will need to be made as to storage of critical resources.

A corollary factor with storage of critical resources is the negative impact of commodity trading. Shortages and delay of materials can have a drastic negative cost effect on industry and other areas of the commercial community. Commodity trading can and does subvert the flow of these materials. Traders can and do manipulate the market, creating unnecessary shortages through price manipulation. Good planning and storage of strategic materials at the national level would help stabilize markets and minimize the impact of this egregious conduct.

Secure storage of critical items to stabilize commercial activity should be a government priority. National stability and efficiency are dependent on a secure and stable flow of materials of every kind.

We are part of a new global community, and though the challenges are great, the opportunities far outweigh the negatives. The United States is still the greatest nation in the world, and by recognizing our flaws and taking constructive action, we can maintain that position. However, to make that happen, citizens must rise to the occasion.

CHAPTER 23

A New Economic Base

What then is the strategy to overcome the current stagnation and rebuild the economy of the Republic? There are two major factors.

Balance is first and foremost. No facet of the community can gain preemptive control. This danger was recognized early on, and commissions were established to guard against such eventualities. However, government failed in enforcement, particularly with regard to the financial community. This was and is a major factor in the current stagnation.

Second is sharing, which is a nice term for taxation. The tax structure has been an abysmal failure. To be realistic, the variables for sharing are almost unfathomable in our legal quagmire and the current tax code. We can fret and whine about it, or we can develop the fairest system possible. Until we can precisely track the wealth and money flow, all sharing judgments will be challenged. Taxing millionaires is a vapid sideshow and political froth. The nation cannot have an adequate sharing method until an accountable financial base is established.

So what is a fair and accountable base for sharing?

What then constitutes an accountable base for sharing? Is it income or wealth? To date, the nation has dealt only with income. Wealth was created originally by conversion of raw materials to products that have more value than the sum of the material and labor involved. Henry Ford and Andrew Carnegie became billionaires through this process, which created hundreds of thousands of jobs. The nation's industrial creativity as well as efficiency gains in both industry and agriculture created the greatest wealth the world has ever known. With great wealth and limited social programs, adequate sharing was possible with income as the basic component.

With the current increase in social programs, that posture is being challenged. The nation has not yet had to address wealth distribution for sharing. However, this has recently become a reality in one nation. In Cyprus, the financial failure of government has required citizen wealth to be assessed or face national bankruptcy. This should be a wake-up call to the citizens of every nation in the world to the potential consequences of fiscal irresponsibility. Unfortunately, the answer to a fair and accountable base for sharing is, (a) we don't know and, (b) we will not know until we gain control of our economic universe. It's as simple as that. The nation's current fragmented financial and economic systems are totally inadequate to meet the need for sharing. Sharing has become a political nightmare creating national gridlock and tearing the nation apart.

Simply stated, a restructuring of the nation's commerce and a new economic base is absolutely necessary before an adequate sharing base can be established.

CHAPTER 24

A New Economic/Systemic View

Economics has been discussed, reviewed and studied since feudalism in China. It was primarily a philosophical exercise until mercantilism, the industrial revolution and capitalism brought economics into more specific focus. Mass production of goods changed nations' socio/economic environments. The current definition of economics is the social science that analyzes production, distribution and consumption of goods and services. The current basic component of economics is money.

Money as the nations' economic base has been a disaster. Our roads and bridges are falling apart. The necessary materials and idle manpower are available but nothing is done. Money, once the means for accumulating wealth, has turned into a destructive force. The inability to manage money has destroyed people, families and even nations. It nearly ruined Greece, and much of the global financial community is in jeopardy.

So how do we use money effectively to support the socio-economic base? While there have been selective gains in economic theory, I could find no examples of any national economy functioning under an accepted set of economic rules. If there were, the United States and many other world nations would be in better economic straits. My background in both Industrial Planning and Information Technology cause me to challenge current economic thinking.

> *My view is that creation of a stable economy strong enough to support the socio-economic community will be achieved only with a planning and control system that balances all the nation's commercial activities from wealth creation to social needs.*

This effectively says that production, distribution and consumption of goods and services is only one element in the creation of a stable economy. All commercial activities should be the base, and a comprehensive system is necessary to provide the tools necessary to achieve balance. To make this systemic view a reality requires an audit-proof commercial base and national planning.

An economic model (actual, not theoretical) of all commercial activity is required. A national planning commission would keep government apprised of the necessary resources for a stable economy: energy, materials, food, etc. et al. They would constantly monitor commercial activity and apprise all users of the state of the state. The goal is to provide the same level of synergy achieved during WWII.

The recommendation for a new economy is based on the above theory. A viable and stable economy will allow our nation to become as efficient as possible. Our standard of living will be the direct result of our endeavors; the value of our currency will stabilize in the world market place; the watered money will dissipate to a realistic level; and our trade with the world community will be based on a solid cost basis. If we are the most efficient nation, our standard of living can improve through international trade. If not, we must live within our means and accept the standard of living our efforts provide.

The nation must have a stable socio/economic system. The boom and bust economy of the past has created havoc. The nation has fallen into debt that it may never be able to repay. The socio/economic system is completely out of balance. Continuation of current economic practices will destroy the Republic.

CHAPTER 25

A New Commercial Base

The government's inability to establish a viable economy and the associated danger of another meltdown point up the critical need for a new economic/commercial system.

To establish a viable economic system, we have to go back to the fundamentals of good money management. There must be balance and control. Laws were passed to prevent the commercial universe from using exploitative and monopolistic practices, but these have not been enforced. In addition to the current stagnation, the result of financial dereliction has been the development of a large underground economy.

The recommended FIX for the economy is creation of a new commercial base, a new financial system that will consolidate the nation's transactions into a single revenue stream.

The strategic objective of the new commercial system is to stabilize the economy with a secure financial base and reverse the current devaluation of the dollar in the world market place.

The operational objective is cost reduction through elimination of waste in both government and private bureaucracies. There are potential cost savings of hundreds of billions of dollars through elimination of waste in these bloated bureaucracies

A secondary operational objective is to bring the large economic underground into the main stream. A recent study estimates that underground activity could amount to over two trillion dollars per year. This again represents hundreds of billions of dollars lost to the nation through tax evasion, fraud and other abuses. This represents another potential bonanza of income for the economy.

The overall objective is to stabilize the nation's economy and provide the maximum level of personal and financial security for its citizens.

What is the design of the new commercial system?

The recommended system is a federal computer-based network within which all the nation's financial transactions would be processed. The communication networks are already in place, and nearly all legal domestic transactions are already being made through these networks.

The commercial universe would see little change. Transactions for receivables and payables would continue as usual. Private citizens would use the system similarly to the way credit card purchases are made today. Every commercial transaction would be networked and available for auditing and legitimacy.

A Federal database would be established for security and control. This database would identify all legal citizen or commercial entities that create financial transactions. The entire nation would be networked, and transactions would be initiated by these legitimate entities. Only they would have access to the nation's commercial base; there would be no access or support for underground activity.

The new system would, for the first time, provide both the institutional government and private citizens with a weekly balance sheet showing the real economic "state of the state". This is the accounting tool that every household or business has needed and used since perpetuity.

Though this would certainly be a massive project, it is do-able with today's technology, and it is unquestionably necessary. It is the answer to the needs of today, but more importantly, it is absolutely critical for the future. Nations of the future will require new and improved systems to optimize their resources and compete in the global marketplace. Those who move forward will be able to maintain their position. Those who do not will fall by the wayside.

The United States is well ahead of the rest of the world in its ability to achieve this goal. We have the necessary physical and technical resources to make a quantum leap in governmental and commercial efficacy. We can do it professionally now at minimum cost and begin reaping the benefits, or we can or let it be another meandering development at multiples of cost and almost certainly additional disasters in effectiveness.

> *Beyond the absolute necessity for such a system, the benefits would be staggering.*

The new system would provide a new level of intelligence to the commercial community. Current financial transactions have only limited intelligence, ie: the purchaser, the provider and a value. The new system would also provide the transaction purpose, ie: payroll, rent, food, tax, commissions—the possibilities are infinite. This new intelligence would provide a revolutionary new dimension in tracking commercial activity. A database showing every detail of commerce would allow economists and planners to optimize every aspect of trade. This area alone would save business of every type hundreds of billions of dollars per year.

Government planners could analyze every dollar spent for government services, enabling substantial cost reductions.

The nation would finally have an adequate base for sharing. The potential for new methods such as a flat tax replacing the current tax code would provide both cost savings and more happy citizens.

The new commercial system would resolve most of the problems of today, but more importantly would be the base for continued growth and development. The future is almost limitless.

Another note of caution, however: savvy readers can see that a similar process could evolve through normal, gradual development. This must be avoided at all cost. Continuation of present practices would result in further exacerbation of the legal quagmire and could well lead to a national disaster. The proposed system is a critical need for the nation; it must be developed professionally with the highest level of technical expertise.

CHAPTER 26

A New Secure Financial Order

The new commercial system would be the initial move toward a cashless society, which is inevitable. Money (script) accounts for less than three percent of the nation's financial activity, and with improved technology that percentage is getting smaller. Script is an archaic impediment. Rolls of script and/or stuffed suitcases open the door to all sorts of undesirable practices; robbery, drug use, gambling, prostitution, underground businesses—the list is endless.

Under the new commercial system, virtually all purchases would take place without script. The purchaser would be linked with the provider through the secure federal database, which would finalize the transaction. There would be no need for either identity cards or script.

The technology to do this is already available and distributable through the internet. Linking the purchaser to the secure federal user database, an absolute necessity, could easily be accomplished using the technique already in use for credit cards.

The federal database of all users would be the most secure in the world. Creation of the database would begin
with the consolidation of all current files, including social
security, health care, etc. et al. The end objective would be
to consolidate all citizen and commercial files into a single
protected database. All rogue files currently in existence
would be eliminated.

This database would be the secure filter which would provide the only access to the financial system. Citizens will
have complete access and finally have control of their own
destiny. They alone would identify who has access to their
files and for what use. Hacking the federal database would
be a major criminal offense subject to a long prison term.

This is not an extreme concept. Citizen databases already
exist in other countries. India is currently developing a per-
sonnel data base for its billion plus citizens, and England is
working on a system to replace checks. The cashless society is the way of the future.

Although limited use of script must be allowed for petty
cash transactions, such use would be sharply curtailed.
Script hoarders would be unhappy, but it is the only way
to guarantee elimination of underground activity. I'm sure
honorable citizens will accept the change when the benefits become obvious.

On a lighter note, casinos will have no objection, since they already function on chips. Floating crap games may have to live with new limits.

The final step in the move to a cashless society would be the issuance of new currency. There would be a one-time house cleaning of current script. For decades, the United State hundred-dollar bill has been the basis for underground activity. It is estimated that (97%) of all hundred-dollar bills ever printed are out of circulation; they are in safety deposit boxes, shoe boxes, suitcases, mattresses, etc.. This should bring about a cash bonanza in income tax revenue as underground briefcases and rolls of the current script are cashed in.

CHAPTER 27

Implementation Concern

It would be disingenuous to say that the new commercial system will be an immediate FIX to all the nation's financial problems. Some immediate steps are necessary. The current stumbling block is the ideological stalemate in Congress, discussed earlier under Institutional Gridlock. Conservatives will not accept tax increases, and liberals will not accept cutbacks in social support. The answer has to be compromise, including a realistic appraisal of our financial condition and constructive efforts for survival. The nation cannot be bankrupted through the intransigence of politicians.

Reason is a nice word. It implies a logical thought process without the definitive restrictions of infallibility. Today there is a new need for reason. There are no guaranteed steps in getting our country through its self-imposed financial crisis. We must make "reasonable" assumptions and take actions with the understanding they might not all work.

We cannot sit on our hands hoping for a miracle. Tough judgments must be made and action steps taken. Further stalling will only exacerbate the problem. The compromise answer must be cost reduction and increased revenue through *whatever* resources are necessary. By biting the bullet, we can avoid bankruptcy, giving ourselves a few years to get our house in order.

Congress is the key player. The Members of Congress are the primary culprits responsible for the mess our nation is in, and they must be the key players in getting us out of it. They were constitutionally assigned primary responsibility for the future of their nation, and they have failed at every turn. They must take action to reconfirm their constitutional role as the primary government power.

If Congress does not take action steps to get the nation back on track, its role will have to be reevaluated. The Republic cannot survive with the poor quality of past congressional performance.

CHAPTER 28

Project Initialization

Design and implementation of the new commercial system will be one of the most significant federal tasks ever undertaken. It will begin the restructuring of the nation's financial universe.

The technology to support a new commercial system is already available, and Congress has the authority to sponsor the project. There will need to be an independent Information Technology task force doing the analytical and design work. The task force will bring the institutional branches into the project, as design decisions need to be made and laws passed to codify them.

The new commercial system will be fought tooth and nail by Wall Street, who will see it as the end of their financial dominance. And members of the Washington establishment would have to finally have to step up and do their jobs.

Most important of all, citizen support to this strategic system is critical.

CHAPTER 29

The Economic Future

What will be the economy of the future?

As was made clear in the previous chapters, the recommended new commercial system will *not* be for the exclusive use of any single commercial entity or industry, including banking. It will be designed to consolidate the nation's financial economy into a single, secure process. It will be a federal system managed and maintained by government. The rules for participation and use will be determined in the network design. New laws will explicitly define the role of every type of user and the transactions allowed to each.

The economy of the future will be logically designed using Information Technology. We used this technology in the 1960's and 70's to improve industrial efficiency, and in spite of institutional stagnation, today's business community has never been healthier. They have two trillion dollars in cash on hand, which they refuse to spend to expand and reduce unemployment. Their rationale is lack of confidence in the institutional government.

The new commercial system will provide the basis for re-structuring the nation's economy. A federal planning commission will use the system for tracking and monitoring economic activity. That function will also provide the planning base so badly needed for governmental funding.

The new federal planning function will provide the tools for effective financial management, from wealth creation to sharing. The institutional government's failure in managing the financial universe was covered earlier. If the institutional government uses this new planning function effectively, the nation's financial health will be improved. If they continue their past politically motivated actions, their inadequacy can be specifically quantified, and citizens can then take the necessary action steps at the next election. There will be no excuses for bad financial management. This will be the final step in eliminating institutional gridlock.

There will need to be a banking function. I know little about banking, but my systemic logic envisions a hierarchy with local banking as a base and a central bank that would oversee all banks within the network. Banks will need to be restricted both geographically and functionally. There must never again be a condition where "too big to fail" can destroy the economy.

Interbank activity must be limited to necessary functional need. Each bank should be a specific legal entity and succeed or perish on its own efficacy. Bailouts open the door to all sorts of chicanery and collusion. Banking would be a community service subject to the same rules as any federal function. Citizen savings should of course be protected under all circumstances.

The nation will finally have the base for a constructive and stable future. A realistic State of the State status can finally be provided at any given time. The political jabberwocky can be replaced with constructive tools to manage the nation on a day-to-day basis while also doing realistic future planning. A fair sharing (tax) base can finally be achieved. There will be no excuses for governmental dereliction. Long term planning on energy and the other resources needed for a stable economy can be achieved. Citizens will finally have confidence in their government.

Having said all that, we need one last note of caution. Citizens have a choice. The economy of the future will be developed, either through a project such as the recommended new commercial system or by default to the haphazard development of the past. There is no possibility for a viable economic system based on legislative laws; that approach has clearly failed, primarily because the need to monitor and control the vast financial universe far exceeds human capabilities.

That vast universe can only be managed using state-of-the-art technology.

CHAPTER 30

USGOV.REBUILD Critique

I hope the reader will reach this point with a positive perspective and a realistic evaluation of the United States Government. The Republic is the best governmental system in the world. That system could continue indefinitely with adequate leadership.

The growth and development of the nation has been a tortuous process consisting primarily of an exploratory exercise. The net result is a mixed bag of procedures and laws that are inhibiting the creation of a stable governmental system. The developing nation has collected a lot of overhead that is not only counter-productive to efficiency but also extremely expensive.

The representative Republic is struggling with a pseudo-monarchy, and citizens' voices are being lost. The pseudo-monarchy is more than executive failure; it is a combination of a vacuous political process and an out-of-control financial community.

Economic failure is resulting in the nation's changing from a three-tiered structure to two: the elite and the poor. The middle class, once the bedrock of the Republic, has been virtually destroyed.

The current cause for failure is of course poor leadership. The political process has produced the most inept set of leaders in the nation's history; and the trend line of incompetence has been drastically accelerated in the new century.

The Washington hierarchy is not capable of FIXES. It will not accept the fact that there is a problem, sweeping it under the rug for political expediency.

Even so, I believe that recovering the founders' vision is possible if concerned citizens recognize the condition and demand that FIXES be made.

FIXING the institutional government cannot wait. The fifty-year erosion cycle is accelerating. The government is very fragile, and continuation of the erosion is untenable.

FIXING the economy is also critical. Our wealth is limited; interest alone on the massive debt accumulated in the new century could bankrupt the nation.

CHAPTER 31

Implementing the FIXES

How do we get the FIXES implemented? FIXES must be based on recognition of the frailty of our government. And we must recognize that no sitting government will *ever* address the issue on its own.

A citizen dialogue is necessary. The best way to start is conversation with friends, neighbors and family. Discuss government as a system. Discuss the current state of the state. Is the current stagnation appearance or substance? Do we have a real problem? Is the problem perhaps overblown, or just the opposite, understated? A realistic appraisal by objective citizens is required before any action plan can be formalized.

Once it is accepted that there is a problem, the basic structure of government should be reviewed. The basis for government is representation. Do we have it or not? Review the FIX on the electoral process. A vote by the citizens of a swing state might be significant. A vote by the citizens of a non-swing state is lost. Has the citizen been disenfranchised by an outmoded and illogical procedure? Representation is the heartbeat of the Republic and should be completely reviewed.

Next, review the Constitution. How does it relate to the real workings of government today? Are the laws we live under true to the Constitution, or are they legislative inter-pretations? Is my earlier reference to the legal quagmire accurate? Congress is a politically organized. Doesn't that automatically introduce ideological bias into our laws?

We hear a lot about the inalienable rights of citizens, but I have not been able to find any reference to those in the Constitution. Why have citizens' Constitutional rights never been legally defined? Shouldn't they be? How about citi-zen responsibilities? Have they ever been defined? If not, why not?

Discussion must be bipartisan. Ideology is the force that determines direction. Conservative and liberal ideologies are positive forces in maintaining balance. However, radi-cal ideology is counterproductive and can promote severe negative consequences.

Extreme conservatism seems to create a rigid and some-time unrealistic fervor. Extreme liberalism seems to pro-mote an unrealistic lack of responsibility and quite often complete rejection of what most citizens consider the norm. The only rationale for discussing ideology is to point out that the governmental system must be functionally transparent. Citizens vote based on their ideology, but the function of government is to allow that freedom without undue influence.

Use the internet as a tool to study. There is a fabulous amount of easily accessible background material. Systemic theory sounds boring, but I urge the reader to give it a chance. For me, studying government has been a fascinating experience, and I think the reader may very well find it equally so.

The last step to discuss here is the first step to be taken: developing a FIXER community.

CHAPTER 32
FIX FIX FIX

The objective of USGOV.FIX and USGOV.REBUILD is to alert citizens to the dangers inherent in the current state of our nation's government and to initiate action steps to get it back on track.

What is the strategy to rebuild the nation? My hope is to use the new social media as a vehicle for change. This can happen if citizens develop discussion groups and discuss the state of the nation. Groups can be expanded as citizens use social media to develop networks across the nation.

I believe the user base should be a somewhat silent majority. Speeches, rallies, street marches and banners are for political fanatics. Fixing government can be accomplished quietly and effectively with a solid base of intelligent citizens.

There will need to be a database of fixers to provide communications and coordination. Limited data should be required; email addresses for fast communication, perhaps State and

Congressional district codes, which would be valuable for statistical analysis. They could also be used for polling.

This is a new and untried effort to improve the governmental system. I have no preconceived ideas as to organization and coordination. We have the most creative people in the world, and I am sure a positive effort can be accomplished. My hope is that citizen dialogues will turn this concept into reality.

I will use my website, USGovfix.com, as a bulletin board and a Facebook page called USGovFix, as a limited blog to further the effort.

Readers must of course make their own judgments as to the criticality of the situation. My systemic evaluation has, I hope, been well stated.

However, if after reading the book the reader does not feel concerned enough to discuss it with others, I do have one suggestion, or perhaps, request; put it down, listen to the news for a week, then pick it back up and re-read it—it will only take an hour. I think after that exercise, you will realize the severity of the problem and begin discussions with other concerned citizens.

In closing, I want to say that I have several beautiful grandchildren and great grandchildren. I cannot bear the thought of their living in a nation less great than the one I fought for. I hope the reader feels the same and will take an active role in rebuilding the Republic.

Thank you for reading my book. Let's start the big FIX.

Yes, Mr. Franklin, we CAN keep it.